GLUTEN-FREE BREAD:

Delicious Easy Homemade Bread

Disclaimer

Introduction

Going gluten-free doesn't have to mean giving up on your favorite breads and biscuits. There are many gluten-free alternatives to all-purpose flour that can be used to make a wide variety of sweet, savory and sandwich breads. Almond flour, coconut flour, tapioca flour and rice flour are just a few of the many options available to you. Used in the right combination with other traditional baking ingredients, you can create gluten-free versions of the breads you love.

Baking gluten-free bread is easier than you might think, especially if you have a good recipe to work with. You may be tempted to take your favorite traditional recipe and simply substitute a gluten-free flour – you may, however, be disappointed. Gluten-free flours do not work in the same way that traditional flours do. You may need to add extra liquid or eggs to the recipe, for example, and you might have to add a binder like xanthan gum to help the ingredients stick together while baking. With practice and a little experimentation, you will have no trouble becoming an excellent gluten-free baker.

If you are new to gluten-free baking some of the ingredients may sound alien to you so I have compiled a list of ingredients used within the book along with a short description. I have included some information and links as to where you can buy.This is just a small compilation and these items are available in numerousstores and online.

Almond flour

Great in gluten-free baking as it adds essential minerals, fiber and protein. It also gives a lovely taste. This is readily available in stores and online.

US Supermarkets, Amazon, Healthy food stores and iHerb

UK Supermarkets including Lidl and TescoAmazoniHerb

Amaranth Flour

Amaranth flour is a protein-rich flour widely used by the Inca and Aztecs. Seeds from the amaranth plant are ground into a fine powder to produce the flour. Although not a grain it produced a grain-like flour gives a nutty and earthy flavor.

USAmazoniHerb, Healthysupplies

UK - Amazon, iHerb

Buckwheat flour

Buckwheat flour is a high protein and mineral flour that gives a brown tint and nut-like earthy taste to bread. It is not a wheat, despite the name, and is in fact related to the rhubarb plant. Buckwheat is available in most supermarkets and health food stores. It is one of my favorites – I like to grind it up buckwheat and make my own flour. You can purchase the pre-made flour if you prefer.

Coconut Flour

Coconut flour is high in fiber, sweet in taste and soaks up a lot of moisture. It works well with eggs in gluten-free recipes. It is available to purchase in most if not all supermarkets and health food stores. You can also make your own as shown in the recipe for coconut mini loaves.

Flaxseed (Linseed)

This is used to give a recipe the elasticity that is missing with the removal of gluten and is readily available in most supermarkets and health stores.

Flax-eggs

In my previous book I gave a link to the blog Bonzai Aphrodite where Sayward details how to makeflax eggs. If you are vegan or have an egg allergy this is a great substitute.

Quinoa Flour (pronounced keen-wa)

Not only is it the oldest cultivated grain in the world, quinoa is also the most nutritious as it is full of iron, calcium and protein. Unlike a lot of gluten-free flours it is does not require a gum, like xanthan or guar, in baking. It is also easy to make your own by rinsing the quinoa in a sieve under cold water. Shake off the excess water and place the quinoa on a baking sheet and bake in an oven for 12-15 minutes at 170C / 350F until dry. Let it cool completely and then grind in a coffee grinder in batches.

Millet flour

Millet flour resembles wheat in texture and appearance. It adds sweetness, nuttiness as well as lightness to baked goods.

US - Bobs Red Mill

UK - Healthysupplies

Oat flour

Oats are a hotly debated subject for those with celiac disease or who are gluten intolerant as they are widely cross contaminated with wheat crops. You need to be certain you are buying 100% gluten-free oats, a few farmers have now started milling gluten-free oats. Bobs Red Mill do a line of gluten-free oats which is available to buy online and in store. Some gluten sensitive people are also sensitive to oats so please ensure you can tolerate them before adding to the recipes.

USAmazon

UKAmazon

Potato Starch

Potato starch is used for its soft, light rise and to add moisture in baking.

US -AmazoniHerb

UK - AmazoniHerb

Sorghum Flour

Sorghum flour is a slightly sweet and soft flour so is great in baking. It is similar to millet flour.

USAmazoniHerb

UK - AmazoniHerb

Tapioca Flour / starch

Tapioca adds texture, structure and gives baked goods a nice chewiness. It is similar to cornflour.

US Amazon iHerb

UKGoodnessdirectAmazoniHerb

Teff

Teff flour is packed full of nutrients and protein. It is also very high in fiber and is thought to help lower blood sugar levels as well as give energy. It has become quite popular with athletes due to its nutritional values. It can be used in place of wheat flour in recipes.

USAmazoniHerb

UKAmazoniHerb

Xanthan Gum

Xanthan gum is used in gluten-free baking to moisten, thicken, bind and pump up the ingredients. It needs to be used correctly as too much can make bread become heavy and taste artificial.

US -The free from or baking aisles in supermarkets, iHerb, Amazon Health stores

UK / IRE / EU - The free from and baking aisles in Supermarkets like Tesco, iHerb and Amazon

For any of you that don't have cups for measurements the following link is a handy resource to find out the weight in grams for the recipes.

Cups to grams

So, what are you waiting for? Gather up your ingredients and let's start baking!

Table of Contents

Sweet Breads

Recipes Included in this Chapter:

Banana Bread

Honey Oat Quick bread

Orange Cranberry Bread

Cinnamon Raisin Bread

Hawaiian Sweet Bread

Banana Bread

Banana Bread is one of those classic recipes that everyone enjoys. If you ever find yourself with a few bananas that are past their prime, you have the perfect excuse to make a loaf of banana bread!

Prep Time: 10 minutes

Cook Time: 55 minutes

Ingredients:

- 1 1/3 cups rice flour
- ½ cup potato starch
- ¼ cup tapioca flour
- 1 teaspoon xanthan gum
- 1 teaspoon baking soda
- ¼ teaspoon sea salt
- 4 large eggs
- 4 medium ripe bananas, mashed
- ½ cup organic honey
- ½ cup unsweetened applesauce
- 1/3 cup unsalted butter, melted
- 1 teaspoon vanilla extract
- 1 cup chopped walnuts plus extra for topping

Directions:

1. Preheat the oven to 180C / 350F and lightly grease two standard loaf pans with cooking spray.

2. Whisk together the flours, xanthan gum, baking soda and salt in a large mixing bowl and add the chopped walnuts

3. In a separate bowl, whisk together the eggs, banana, sugar, applesauce, butter and vanilla extract.

4. Add the wet ingredients to the dry and blend until just combined.

5. Divide the batter evenly between the two pans and spread evenly. Sprinkle with extra walnuts if desired

6. Bake for 45 to 55 minutes until a knife inserted in the center comes out clean.

7. Cool the loaves for 10 minutes in the pan then turn out onto a wire rack to cool completely.

Honey Oat Quick bread

As explained in the flour section, while oats themselves do not contain gluten, they are often processed on the same equipment that processes wheat. This being the case, you need to be careful to purchase "gluten-free oats"

Prep Time: 1 hour

Cook Time: 45 minutes

Ingredients:

- 4 cups gluten-free oats (plus extra for topping)
- 2 tablespoons active dry yeast
- 1 ½ cups warm water
- ¼ cup olive oil
- 1/3 cup honey
- ½ cup tapioca starch

- ½ cup sweet rice flour

- 2 teaspoons xanthan gum

- 1 teaspoon sea salt

- ¼ teaspoon ground cinnamon

- 4 large eggs

Directions:

1. Preheat the oven to 180C / 350F and grease a standard loaf pan with cooking spray.

2. Place the oats in a food processor and blend until finely powdered.

3. In a small bowl, whisk together the yeast and water and let sit for 5 minutes or so.

4. Whisk together the oil, honey, tapioca starch, rice flour, xanthan gum and powdered oats in a mixing bowl until well combined.

5. Add the yeast mixture and blend until smooth.

6. Beat in the salt, cinnamon and eggs until the mixture is fluffy.

7. Transfer the dough into the prepared pan and let rise for 45 minutes until about doubled in size.

8. Sprinkle the top of the loaf with whole oats and score the top with a serrated knife.

9. Bake for 45 minutes then cool in the pan for 10 minutes. Turn out onto a wire rack to cool completely.

Orange Cranberry Bread

The best thing about this recipe – besides the fact that it is easy to prepare – is that you can customize it however you like. Substitute the orange zest for lemon or the cranberries for chopped dried apricots and you have an entirely new recipe!

Prep Time: 15 minutes

Cook Time: 1 hour

Ingredients:

- ½ cup unsalted butter, softened
- 1 cup plus 1 tablespoon white sugar
- 1 ½ cups rice flour
- ½ cup potato starch
- 1/3 cup tapioca flour
- 1 tablespoon fresh orange zest
- 1 teaspoon xanthan gum
- 1 teaspoon baking powder
- ½ teaspoon baking soda
- ½ teaspoon sea salt
- 10 ounces fresh cranberries, halved
- 2/3 cup unsweetened almond milk, room temperature
- ¼ cup sour cream, room temperature
- Extra sugar (optional)

Directions:

1. Preheat the oven to 180C / 350F and lightly grease a standard loaf pan.

2. Beat the butter in the bowl of a stand mixer until light and fluffy. Add 1 cup sugar and eggs, beating well.

3. In a mixing bowl, blend the flours, xanthan gum, orange zest, baking powder, baking soda and salt until well combined.

4. Place the cranberries in a small bowl and toss with about 1 tablespoon of the blended dry ingredients and the remaining 1 tablespoons sugar.

5. Add the dry ingredients to the bowl of the stand mixer in small batches, alternating with the milk and sour cream. Beat until well combined.

6. Fold in the cranberries

7. Transfer the batter to the prepared pan and smooth out the top. Sprinkle the top lightly with sugar, if desired.

8. Bake for 1 hour until a knife inserted in the center comes out clean.Remove from the oven and cool for 20 minutes in the pan before turning out onto a wire rack to cool completely.

Cinnamon Raisin Bread

Included in this recipe is a bonus recipe for making your own all-purpose gluten-free flour blend. Make some extra to keep on hand for use in other recipes!

Prep Time: 1 hour

Cook Time: 55 minutes

Ingredients:

- 1 ½ cups sorghum flour
- 1 ½ cups millet flour
- 1 cup tapioca flour
- 1 cup potato starch
- 1 cup arrowroot powder
- 4 teaspoons xanthan gum

- 1 teaspoon sea salt

- ¼ cup honey

- 2 teaspoon dry active yeast

- 2 teaspoon ground cinnamon

- 4 teaspoons coconut oil, melted

- 3 ½ cups warm water

- 1 ½ cups raisins

Directions:

1. Preheat the oven to 100C / 200F then grease and flour two standard loaf pans.

2. Create your flour mix by blending the millet flour, sorghum flour, tapioca flour, potato starch and arrowroot powder in a mixing bowl.

3. Blend until well combined then set aside 1 cup of the mixture for future use (you do not need it for this recipe).

4. Add the xanthan gum, salt, yeast and cinnamon to the flour mixture and blend until well combined.

5. Whisk together the coconut oil, honey and warm water in the bowl of a stand mixer then blend in the dry ingredients in small batches.

6. Blend the mixture on high speed for 2 minutes to activate the yeast. Fold in the raisins by hand.

7. Divide the batter evenly between the two pans and cover lightly with clean tea towels.

8. Turn off the oven and set the pans inside to rise for about 30 minutes. Remove the bread from the oven and set aside.

9. Reheat the oven to 200C / 400F then bake the bread for 50 to 55 minutes. After the first 15 minutes, gently place a tent of foil over the bread to prevent the crust from burning.

10. Cool the bread for 10 minutes in the pans then turn out onto a wire rack to cool completely.

Hawaiian Sweet Bread

This Hawaiian Sweet Bread is light and sweet, the perfect bread to enjoy with jam at breakfast or as an afternoon snack.

Prep Time: 1 hour

Cook Time: 45 minutes

Ingredients:

- Cooking spray
- ½ cup warm water
- 2 teaspoons white sugar, divided
- ¼ cup honey
- 2 ½ teaspoons active dry yeast
- 2 cups brown rice flour
- ½ cup tapioca flour
- ½ cup potato starch
- 1 tablespoon xanthan gum
- 1 teaspoon sea salt
- 3 tablespoons unsalted butter, melted
- 3 large eggs
- ½ cup warm almond milk

Directions:

1. Preheat oven to 180C / 350F and lightly grease a

standard loaf pan with cooking spray.

2. Whisk together the water, 2 teaspoons sugar and yeast in a small bowl. Stir until dissolved then set aside, covered with a clean towel, for 10 minutes.

3. Combine the dry ingredients in the bowl of a food processor and blend for 2 to 3 minutes until well combined.

4. In a mixing bowl, whisk together the melted butter, honey, eggs and milk until smooth.

5. Add the wet ingredients to the dry ingredients and blend until well combined. Add the yeast mixture and blend until a soft dough forms.

6. Turn the dough out into the prepared pan and smooth the top with a wet spatula.

7. Set the pan in a warm area to rise for about 40 minutes.

8. Lightly score the top of the loaf with a sharp knife then bake for 40 to 45 minutes until the internal temperature reaches about 195°F.

9. Let the loaf cool for 5 to 10 minutes in the pan then turn out onto a wire rack to cool completely.

Savory Breads

Recipes Included in this Chapter:

Zucchini Bread

Rice Flour Mini Rolls

Garlic and Onion Dinner Rolls

Coconut Mini Loaves

Vegan Rosemary Bread

Buttermilk Biscuits

Buckwheat and Almond Bread

Soda Bread

Chickpea and Quinoa Bread

Zucchini Bread

What keeps this bread moist and flavorful is the fresh grated zucchini. Not only does the zucchini give this bread a unique flavor, but it also improves the nutrient content!

Prep Time: 15 minutes

Cook Time: 50 minutes

Ingredients:

- ¾ cups sorghum flour
- ¾ cups millet flour
- ½ cup tapioca flour
- ½ cup potato starch
- ½ cup arrowroot powder
- 1 teaspoon xanthan gum
- 1 teaspoon sea salt
- 1 teaspoon baking soda
- 1 teaspoon baking powder
- 2 ½ teaspoons ground cinnamon
- ½ cup light brown sugar, packed
- 2 ½ cups grated zucchini (excess liquid squeezed out)
- 3 large eggs, beaten
- 1 ripe banana, mashed
- ½ cup canola oil

- 1 ½ teaspoons vanilla extract

Directions:

1. Preheat the oven to 165C / 325F and grease two standard loaf pans.

2. Combine the flours, xanthan gum, salt, baking soda, baking powder, cinnamon and sugar in a mixing bowl.

3. Whisk the mixture until well combined then set aside.

4. In a separate mixing bowl, whisk together the zucchini, eggs, banana, oil and vanilla extract. Stir well.

5. Create a well in the center of the dry ingredients and add the wet ingredients in a single batch.

6. Stir until the ingredients are just combined and the batter is free from lumps.

7. Divide the batter evenly between the two pans and smooth the tops using a spatula.

8. Bake for 45 to 50 minutes, rotating the pans once halfway through, until a knife inserted in the center comes out clean.

9. Cool the bread in the pans for 10 minutes then turn out onto a wire rack to cool completely.

Rice Flour Mini Rolls

These rice flour mini rolls are easy to throw together and are the perfect accompaniment for nearly any meal. Feel free to sweeten them with a drizzle of honey or a little brown sugar, if you like!

Prep Time: 15 minutes

Cook Time: 25 minutes

Ingredients:

- ¾ cup warm water
- 1 ½ teaspoons active dry yeast
- 1 cup brown rice flour
- ¼ cup tapioca starch
- ¼ cup potato starch
- 1 teaspoon xanthan gum
- ½ teaspoon sea salt
- 3 tablespoons extra-virgin olive oil
- 2 large eggs, lightly beaten
- ½ teaspoon cider vinegar

Directions:

1. Preheat the oven to 190C / 375F and lightly grease a standard muffin pan.

2. Combine the water and yeast in a small bowl. Stir until

the yeast is dissolved then cover with a towel and set aside for 10 minutes.

3. Combine the rice flour, tapioca starch, potato starch, xanthan gum and salt in the bowl of a stand mixer. Blend well.

4. In a mixing bowl, whisk together the olive oil, eggs and vinegar until smooth.

5. Add the olive oil mixture and the yeast mixture to the dry ingredients and beat until well combined.

6. Continue to beat the mixture on medium speed for 2 to 3 minutes until the dough is sticky and soft.

7. Scoop the dough into the prepared muffin pan and place in a warm area to rise for 20 to 25 minutes until almost doubled in size.

8. Bake for 20 to 25 minutes until lightly browned and crusty on top.

Garlic and Onion Dinner Rolls

These dinner rolls are easy to prepare and can be customized to suit your taste. Though this recipe calls for the flavors of garlic and onion, you can also add rosemary or other dried herbs for flavor.

Prep Time: 15 minutes

Cook Time: 20 minutes

Ingredients:

- ¾ cup hot water
- 1 tablespoon honey
- 2 ¼ teaspoons active dry yeast
- 1 cup sorghum flour
- ¾ cup millet flour
- 1 ¾ teaspoons xanthan gum
- 1 ¼ teaspoons sea salt
- 2 tablespoons dehydrated onion flakes
- 2 cloves garlic, minced
- 1 teaspoon onion powder
- 2 large eggs, lightly beaten
- 2 tablespoons olive oil
- ½ teaspoon cider vinegar

Directions:

1. Combine the hot water, honey and yeast in a small bowl. Stir briefly then let sit for 7 minutes.

2. Combine the sorghum flour, millet flour, tapioca starch, xanthan gum and sea salt in a mixing bowl.

3. Add the minced garlic, dehydrated onion flakes and onion powder then stir until well combined.

4. In a separate bowl, whisk together the eggs, oil and vinegar. Add the egg mixture to the dry ingredients and stir well.

5. Add the yeast mixture to the batter and blend until smooth and well combined.

6. Scrape down the sides of the bowl then beat the mixture on medium speed for 2 to 3 minutes until the dough is smooth – you may need to add a few tablespoons of water.

7. Use an ice cream scoop to drop the dough onto a parchment-lined baking sheet – the dough should divide evenly into 12 scoops.

8. Shape the rolls into the desired shape and lightly flatten each roll to about 1 inch thickness.

9. Let the rolls rise for 20 minutes in a warm area and preheat the oven to 180C / 375F.

10. Bake for 18 to 20 minutes until golden brown on top.

11. Let the rolls cool in the pan for 5 minutes then remove to a wire rack to cool completely before serving.

Coconut Mini Loaves

In this recipe you essentially make your own coconut flour by grinding flaked / desiccated coconut into a powder. This is a useful tip if you ever find yourself without coconut flour for future recipes. This bread can be savory or sweet, add honey for a sweeter bread. Once cooled and sliced this can also be made in to gorgeous French toast.

Prep Time: 10 minutes

Cook Time: 35 minutes

Ingredients:

- 3 large eggs, lightly beaten

- 2 egg whites, lightly beaten

- 2 tablespoons natural yogurt

- 3 cups unsweetened flaked coconut

- 1 teaspoon baking powder

- 3 tablespoons honey (optional – if you would like a sweeter bread)

Directions:

1. Preheat the oven to 180C / 350F and lightly grease two mini loaf pans.

2. Beat together the eggs, yogurt and honey if using in a medium mixing bowl.

3. Place the coconut flakes in a food processor and blend until finely powdered – do not over-blend.

4. Add the powdered coconut and baking powder to the egg mixture and blend until smooth. The consistency should be cake-like but not too wet.

5. Divide the batter between the two loaf pans and bake for 18 minutes.

6. Open the oven door and let the oven temperature drop to about 150C / 300F.

7. Bake the loaves for another 10 to 15 minutes until a skewer inserted in the center comes out clean.

8. Cool the loaves in the pans for 5 minutes then turn out onto a wire rack to cool completely.

Vegan Rosemary Bread

This recipe is considered both gluten-free and vegan because it uses ground flaxseed as a substitute for eggs. You can also use Ener-G egg replacer, if you prefer.

Prep Time: 15 minutes

Cook Time: 40 minutes

Ingredients:

- 6 tablespoons warm water
- ½ cup ground flaxseed
- ½ cup coconut flour
- 1 tablespoon dried rosemary
- ½ tablespoon dried thyme
- 1 ½ teaspoons baking soda
- ¼ teaspoon sea salt
- ¼ cup coconut oil, melted
- 1 tablespoon cider vinegar

Directions:

1. Preheat the oven to 165C / 325F and lightly grease a loaf pan.

2. Whisk together the water and flaxseed in a small bowl then set aside.

3. Combine the coconut flour, rosemary, thyme, baking soda and salt in a mixing bowl and stir well.

4. In a separate bowl mix the coconut oil and cider vinegar.

5. Add the wet ingredients to the dry ingredients along with the water and flaxseed mixture.

6. Stir until well combined in a smooth batter.

7. Pour the batter into the loaf pan and spread evenly.

8. Bake for 35 to 40 minutes until a knife inserted in the center comes out clean.

9. Cool the bread for 10 minutes in the pan then transfer to a wire rack to cool completely.

Buttermilk Biscuits / Scones

Buttermilk biscuits, or scones as they are called in England and Ireland, are the perfect savory or sweet snack. Spread them with a little warm butter and cheese for savory or strawberry jam and cream and you'll be in sweet heaven!

Prep Time: 10 minutes

Cook Time: 15 minutes

Ingredients:

- ½ cup white rice flour
- ½ cup gluten-free oat flour
- ½ cup tapioca starch
- ¼ cup coconut flour
- 1 tablespoon cornstarch
- 3 teaspoons xanthan gum

- 2 teaspoons baking powder

- ½ teaspoon baking soda

- 1 teaspoon sea salt

- ¼ cup unsalted butter, chopped

- 1 cup buttermilk

- ¼ cup natural yogurt

Directions:

1. Preheat the oven to 190C / 375F.

2. Combine the flours, xanthan gum, baking powder, baking soda and salt in a mixing bowl and stir well.

3. Cut in the butter using a pastry cutter until it forms a crumbly mixture.

4. Add the buttermilk and yogurt to the dry ingredients and blend until just combined.

5. Turn the dough out onto a floured surface and pat it into a disc shape about 1 inch thick.

6. Use a round biscuit cutter to cut the biscuits and arrange them on a parchment-lined baking sheet. Make sure to use up all the dough.

7. Brush the tops of the biscuits lightly with milk and bake for 11 to 14 minutes until the tops are lightly browned.

Buckwheat and Walnut Bread

This is my favorite bread recipe from the entire book. I adore the texture, flavor and the fact that you can change the nuts and seeds to whatever you have to hand. Substitute hazelnuts for the walnuts or pumpkins seeds for sunflower seeds.

Prep Time: 10 minutes

Cook Time: 50 minutes

Ingredients:

- 1 ½ cup buckwheat flour
- 1 cup almond flour
- 1 tablespoon baking powder
- ¼ cup walnuts – roughly chopped
- Handful sunflower seeds

- 3 tablespoons natural yogurt

- 1 ¾ cup of buttermilk

- 1 teaspoon treacle

- 1 teaspoon honey

Directions:

1. Pre-heat your oven to 200C / 380F and grease a bread tin

2. In a bowl combine the buckwheat flour, almond flour, walnuts and baking powder

3. Make a well in the center and add the yogurt, honey and buttermilk

4. Add the sunflower seeds and treacle

5. Pour the mixture in to the bread tin and bake for 35 minutes

6. Check to make sure the top is not burning, if it is cover with foil before returning back to the oven for 15 minutes

7. Remove from the oven and insert a skewer to check if it is done. Leave in the tin for 10 minutes before putting on to a wire rack to cool completely before slicing

Soda Bread

This is a lovely light bread due to the egg whites and yogurt. It would be great with a bowl of soup or served with a hearty stew.

Prep Time: 10 minutes

Cook Time: 60 minutes

Ingredients:

- ½ cup buckwheat flour
- 1 ½ cup sorghum flour
- 3 teaspoons baking powder
- ½ teaspoon salt
- 2 tablespoons mixed seeds
- ¼ cup natural yogurt
- 1cup of low fat milk
- 2 egg whites
- 1 teaspoon honey

Directions:

1. Pre-heat oven to 180C / 350F and spray / grease your bread tin

2. Put the flours and salt in to a bowl and sift in the baking powder

3. Whish the two egg whites with an electric mixer until they are light and fluffy. Add the honey, milk and yogurt

and stir to combine

4. Pour the batter in to the pre-greased bread tin and top with the mixed seeds patting them onto the top with a spatula

5. Bake for an hour and check if it's done by inserting a skewer – if it comes out clean it is cooked

6. Leave in the bread tin for 10 minutes before removing to a wire rack. Let it cool completely before slicing

Chickpea & Quinoa Bread

Chick peas and quinoa are two of my favorite ingredients and they work a treat in this bread! Serve with homemade pate or hummus for the extra chickpea flavor.

Prep Time: 10 minutes

Cook Time: 45 minutes

Ingredients:

- 1 cup buckwheat flour

- 1 cup quinoa flour (see note in flour)

- 1 teaspoons baking powder

- ½ teaspoon baking soda

- ½ teaspoon salt

- 1 ¼ buttermilk

- 1 can chickpeas (drained and rinsed)

- 1 flax egg - 3 tablespoons warm water &1 tablespoon flax meal

Directions:

1. Pre-heat your oven to 180C / 350F and grease your bread tin

2. Mix the warm water with the flax meal to make your flax egg and leave to set.

3. Place the drained chickpeas and ¼ cup buttermilk in to a food processor and blend until smooth

4. Place the buckwheat, quinoa, baking powder and baking soda in to a bowl

5. Mix the flax egg, honey, chickpea mixture and remaining buttermilk

6. Pour the chickpea mixture in to the dry ingredients and mix well to combine

7. Scrape the mixture from the bowl with a spatula and pour in to your bread tin

8. Bake for 45 minutes, check by inserting a skewer in to the center of the loaf. Once clean it is cooked. Leave in the bread tin for 10 minutes before removing and letting cool on a wire rack.

Sandwich Breads

Recipes Included in this Chapter:

Almond Sandwich Bread

White Sandwich Bread

Simple Brown Bread

Pita Bread

Multigrain Sandwich Bread

Almond Sandwich Bread

This sandwich bread is topped with sliced almonds for a little bit of added crunch. If you like the flavor of almonds but not the texture, feel free to omit them from the recipe – you will still get plenty of almond flavor from the almond flour.

Prep Time: 15 minutes

Cook Time: 30 minutes

Ingredients:

- 2 cups almond flour
- 2 tablespoons coconut flour
- ¼ cup ground flaxseed
- ½ teaspoon baking soda
- ½ teaspoon sea salt
- 5 large eggs, lightly beaten

- 1 tablespoon coconut oil, melted

- 1 teaspoon honey

- 1 teaspoon cider vinegar

- 2 tablespoons sliced almonds

Directions:

1. Preheat the oven to 180C / 350F and lightly grease a standard loaf pan.

2. Combine the almond flour, coconut flour, ground flaxseed, baking soda and salt in a mixing bowl.

3. In a separate bowl, beat together the eggs, honey, oil and vinegar.

4. Add the wet ingredients to the dry and beat until smooth and well combined.

5. Pour the batter into the prepared pan and sprinkle with sliced almonds.

6. Bake for 30 to 35 minutes until a knife inserted in the center comes out clean.

7. Cool the bread in the pan for 5 minutes then turn out onto a wire rack to cool completely.

White Sandwich Bread

This white sandwich bread has delicious flavor and a pleasant texture – everything you need to build the perfect sandwich. As an added bonus, it is also dairy-free and rice-free.

Prep Time: 15 minutes

Cook Time: 55 minutes

Ingredients:

- 1 ½ cups sorghum flour
- 1 cup tapioca starch
- ½ cup gluten-free oat flour
- 2 teaspoons xanthan gum
- 1 ¼ teaspoons sea salt
- 1 cup warm water
- 3 teaspoons honey, divided
- 2 ¼ teaspoons active dry yeast
- 3 tablespoons olive oil
- ½ teaspoon fresh lemon juice
- 2 large eggs, lightly beaten

Directions:

1. Combine the warm water with the yeast and 1 teaspoon of honey in a small bowl. Whisk until the yeast is dissolved then let sit for 10 minutes.

2. Whisk together the sorghum flour, tapioca starch, oat flour, xanthan gum and sea salt in a mixing bowl until well combined.

3. Add the yeast mixture to the dry ingredients along with the olive oil, eggs, lemon juice and the remaining honey.

4. Beat the mixture until a smooth batter forms – add up to ¼ cup more warm water, if needed.

5. Transfer the batter to a lightly greased loaf pan and set aside to rise for 45 to 50 minutes.

6. Preheat the oven to 180C / 350F then bake the bread for 45 to 55 minutes until it sounds hollow when thumped.

7. Cool the bread for 10 minutes in the pan then transfer to a wire rack to cool completely.

Simple Brown Bread

If you don't have any all-purpose gluten-free flour on hand, use the ingredients in the Cinnamon Raisin Bread recipe to create your own!

Prep Time: 15 minutes

Cook Time: 45 minutes

Ingredients:

- Cooking spray

- 2 ½ cup gluten-free all-purpose flour blend

- ½ cup oat flour

- 3 tablespoons whole grain teff

- 3 teaspoons active dry yeast

- 1 ¼ teaspoons xanthan gum

- ¼ teaspoon cream of tartar

- ¼ teaspoon baking soda

- 1 ½ teaspoons sea salt

- ¼ cup unsalted butter, softened

- 1 tablespoon vegetable shortening

- 1 tablespoon molasses or honey

- 1 teaspoon cider vinegar

- 2 large egg whites, beaten well

- 1 ½ cups unsweetened almond milk, warm

Directions:

1. Preheat the oven to 190C / 375F and grease a standard loaf pan with cooking spray.

2. Combine the flours, xanthan gum, cream of tartar, yeast and baking soda in the bowl of a stand mixer.

3. Whisk the mixture well then add the salt and blend until well combined.

4. In a separate bowl, whisk together the butter, shortening, vinegar, molasses, egg whites and milk. Blend until smooth.

5. Add the wet ingredients to the dry and beat on low speed until it forms a smooth dough.

6. Cover the bowl of the mixer with a towel and beat on high speed for 5 minutes until the dough is thick.

7. Transfer the dough to the loaf pan and cover with

plastic wrap. Let rise in a warm area until nearly doubled in size.

8. Remove the plastic wrap and bake for 30 minutes until the crust is firm.

9. Carefully remove the loaf from the pan and place it on a baking sheet. Bake for another 5 to 10 minutes until the crust is brown.Let the bread cool for 10 minutes on the baking sheet then transfer to a wire rack to cool completely.

French Bread Loaf

Prep Time: 15 minutes

Cook Time: 45 minutes

Ingredients:

- ¾ cups sorghum flour
- ¾ cups millet flour
- ½ cup tapioca flour
- ½ cup potato starch
- ½ cup arrowroot powder
- 1 tablespoon active dry yeast
- 2 ¼ teaspoons xanthan gum
- 2 teaspoons sea salt
- ½ teaspoon cream of tartar
- 2 extra-large egg whites
- 1 2/3 cups warm water
- 2 tablespoons unsalted butter, softened

Directions:

1. Combine the flours, potato starch, arrowroot powder, yeast, xanthan gum, salt and cream of tartar in the bowl.

2. Whisk until well combined then add the egg whites and blend well.

3. Slowly add the water in a steady stream while mixing with a whisk or spoon. Stop when the dough just begins to come together.

4. Scrape the dough together with a spatula and turn it out onto a piece of parchment paper (un-floured).

5. Knead the dough briefly then divide into two parts.

6. Roll each piece of dough into a cylinder by rolling it back and forth – it will have cracks in it, but that is ok.

7. Dip your hands in warm water and rub the dough until smooth.

8. Place the two pieces of dough about 2 inches apart on a parchment-lined baking sheet and cover with plastic wrap.

9. Let the dough rise for 45 minutes until almost doubled.

10. Meanwhile, preheat the oven to 190C / 375F.

11. Remove the plastic wrap and bake the dough for 15 minutes.

12. Rub the unsalted butter over the surface of the loaves and bake for another 10 to 15 minutes until golden brown.

13. Cool the bread completely on a wire rack before slicing.

Pita Bread

You may have a difficult time finding gluten-free pita bread in the store but don't worry! This recipe makes it easy for you to bake your own pita bread right at home.

Prep Time: 5 minutes

Cook Time: 20 minutes

Ingredients:

- 1 large egg
- ¼ cup warm water
- 1 tablespoon olive oil
- ¼ cup almond flour
- 1/8 teaspoon baking soda
- Pinch sea salt

Directions:

1. Preheat the oven to 180C / 350F and line a baking sheet with parchment paper.

2. Combine the eggs, oil and water in a mixing bowl.

3. In a separate bowl, combine the almond flour, baking soda and salt.

4. Add the dry ingredients to the wet ingredients and blend until well combined – the mixture will be liquid.

5. Carefully pour the mixture onto the baking sheet in two round, even portions.

6. Spread the batter carefully so it bakes evenly.

7. Bake for 18 to 20 minutes until the pita is puffed and lightly browned on the edges.

Multigrain Sandwich Bread

This multigrain sandwich bread is made with half a dozen different kinds of gluten-free flour. If you want to add a little bit extra, sprinkle some sesame seeds and poppy seeds on top of the loaf just before baking.

Prep Time: 15 minutes

Cook Time: 30 minutes

Ingredients:

- 1 cup hot water
- 2 tablespoons honey
- 2 ¼ teaspoons active dry yeast
- 1 cup tapioca flour
- 1 cup millet flour
- ½ cup almond flour
- ½ cup amaranth flour
- ¼ cup sorghum flour
- ¼ cup ground flaxseed
- 2 ¾ teaspoons xanthan gum
- 1 ½ teaspoons sea salt
- 3 large eggs
- 3 tablespoons coconut oil, melted
- 1 tablespoon molasses

- 1 teaspoon cider vinegar

Directions:

1. Whisk together the hot water, honey and yeast in a small bowl then set it aside for 7 minutes to proof.

2. Combine the flours, ground flaxseed, xanthan gum and salt in the bowl of a stand mixer. Blend until well combined.

3. In a separate bowl, beat together the eggs, coconut oil, molasses and cider vinegar.

4. Add the wet ingredients to the dry and beat smooth then beat in the yeast mixture until it forms a sticky dough.

5. Beat the mixture on medium speed for 2 to 3 minutes until the dough is smooth – you may need to scrape the sides several times.

6. Transfer the dough to a grease loaf pan and cover with plastic wrap. Set in a warm location to rise for 45 minutes or so.

7. Pre-heat your oven to 180C / 350F. Remove the plastic wrap and bake for 30 minutes until a knife inserted in the center comes out clean.

8. Turn the loaf out onto a wire rack to cool completely before   slicing.

Conclusion

After reading this book you should have a good idea what it means to be a gluten-free baker. In short, it means that you are creative in using gluten-free alternatives to traditional flour to create delicious gluten-free masterpieces. Hopefully in trying out the recipes in this book you have found a few that you enjoy and you will make them a part of your baking routine. Don't settle for store-bought gluten-free breads that crumble or go bad within a few days – keep yourself stocked with fresh, homemade bread using the recipes in this book!

Thanks for reading and check out my other gluten-free recipe book!

Gluten-free Vegan: Healthy everyday dishes in under 30 minutes

What did you like about the book? Please let me know by leaving a review on amazon.

If you wish to contact me my email address is glutenfreesophie@gmail.com